I0435811

100's Vintage Botany Botanicals, Volume 3 (Floral Ephemera Series 3)
By C. Anders

This book is a work of non-fiction. Images in this book may have been retouched. No part of this book maybe be reproduced, scanned, or printed in any printed or electronic form without permission from the author. Please do not participate or encourage piracy of copyrighted materials in violation of the author's rights.
Purchase only authorized editions.
Copyright © 2019 by C Anders. All rights reserved.

Tab. 38.

Classis XIII. POLYANDRIA VIELFÆDICHTE, B.C.D.E. Di-Tri-Penta-Polygynia.

Tab. 45.

Classis XVI. MONADELPHIA EINSAVLIGE, Plantæ MALVACEÆ PAPPELKRÆVTER.

A. Pentandriæ. Fünffædichte.

Waltheria. Betonien Pappel. 742. Hermania. Schnecken-Pappel. 743.

Pentandr. 747 Melochia. Juden pappel. Decandriæ. Zehenfædichte. Hugonia. Hirschen Pappel. 745. Conarus Klee-Pappel 744.

Geranium √ Decandr.

Sida. Samt-Pappel. 747. C. Polyandriæ. Vielfædichte. 750. Alcea. Saat-Rose. Napæa Napf-Pappel. 748. Lavatera. Lavater-Bluhm Deckel Pappel. 752.

Malva Kasle Kraut. 751. 749 Althæa. Eibisch. Gossypium. Wollen-Staude. 755. Bombax. Baum-Volle. 760.

Malope. Pappel-Beere. 753.

Vrena. Kletten-Pappel. 754.

Hibiscus. Sigmars-Kraut. 756. Pentapetes Flügel-Pappel. 757. Dodecandria! Camellia. Japonesischer Pappelbaum. 759. Stewartia. Virginischer-Pappel-Baum. 758.

Turnera. Sonnen-Pappel. v. 3. 338.

Helicteres Isora. Schrauben Staude. XX. 10. 917.

Tab. 48.

Classis XIX. SYNGENESIA. ZUSAMMENGEWACHSENE. Polygamia æqualis. CICHORACEÆ. WEGWARTKRÄUTER.

810. Tragopogon. Habermark. 3. 904. Geropogon. 811. Scorzonera. Scorzonere.

812. Picris. Gelb Ochsen Zung. 813. Sonchus. Hasen Kohl. 814. Lactuca. Salat. 915. Chondrilla. Gelb wegware.

816. Prenanthes. Bergsaltich. 817. Leontodon. Pfaffen Röhlein. 818. Hieracium. Habicht-Kraut. 819. Crepis. Glatt Habicht Kraut.

820. Andryala. Beth Kraut. 821. Hyoseris. Leuen Fahn. 822. Hypochœris. Forckel Kraut. 823. Lapsana. Wartzen Kohl.

824. Catananche. Buhl Kraut. 826. Scolymus. Gold Distel. 825. Cichorium. Wegwart. 827. Elephantopus. Elephanten Fuss. Polyg. Segreg.

C. G. Geissler del. et Sculps.   Add. Seriola T. 93.

Tab. 4.

Classis III. TRIANDRIA. A. Monogynia. a. Floribus spathaceis triloculares

33. Crocus.   Saffran.
415. VI. 3.   3. DENVDATE et variae SAFFRAN KR.
Colchicum. Zeitlosen Licht-Blume.   Bulbocodium Gelbe Licht-Blume.
366. VI.
Xyris. Gras-Lilie.
259.
Aphyllanthes Blaue Nel.
369. VI.

Eriocaulon. Randu Knopf Gras.
95.

Ixia. Ixie. Chineser Lilie.
54.
2. ENSATE SCHWERTELKRÆVTER.
55. Gladiolus.   Feder-Lilie.
56. Antholyza. Æthiopsche Lilie.
Comelina. Comeline. 58.
Bermudiana.
Berma dische Lilie. god. Sisynrichium.
XX.

57. Iris.   Schwert-Lilie.

C. C. Geyssler. Pinx. et sc. ENSATIS add. Wachendorfia T. 64. Moræa T. 73. Callisia T. 65. Tradescantia, Pontederia T. 23. Ferraria T. 76.

Tab. 11.

Classis V. PENTANDRIA *FÜNF-FÆDICHTE* A Monogynia a Monopetale Trispermæ ASPERIFOLIÆ BORAGINEÆ *BORRETSCH-KRAUTER*

164. Heliotropium *Sonnen-Wendel* · 165. Myosotis *Blauer-Augentrost* · 166. Lithospermum *Steinhirse* · 167. Anchusa *Ochsen-Zunge* · 169. Pulmonaria *Lungen-Kraut*

168. Cynoglossum *Hunds-Zunge* · 170. Symphytum *Wallwurtz* · 171. Cerinthe *Flecken-Kraut* · 172. Borrago *Borretsch*

173. Asperugo *Greau-Kleb-Kraut* · 173. Echium *Blaur-Ochsen-Zunge* · 174. Lycopsis *Wolfs-Zunge* · 176. Tournefortia *Vittonia* · 167. Hydrophyllum *Wasser-blatt*

Tab 2

Classis II. DIANDRIA *ZWEYFÄDICHTE* A. Monogynia. I Corollis regular. SEPIARIÆ. *ZAUSS-GEWÄCHSE*

16. Nyctanthes   *Nacht-blum.   Arabischer Jasmin.*   17.   *Iasminum   Jasmin.*

Gardenia
floridа
V. I
290

18. Ligustrum *Hartriegel Rosengorten*   19. Phillyrea   *Wotsohe-Linde.*   20. Olea   *Oel baum.*   22. Syringa *Lilac Spanisches Holand*

21. Chionanthus   *Sohnee-blum.*   1026.   Fraxinus   *Esch-baum XXIII. 2.*   230. Brunfelsia   *Brunfelsie.*   V. I.

Tab. 57

Classis **XX.** GYNANDRIA *KOLBENFÆDIGE* A. Diandria ORCHIDEÆ. *STENDEL-KRÄUTER*

900. Orchis Stendelwurz

901. Satyrium Mechvle

902. Ophris Vogelnest

903. Serapias Helleborine

904. Limodorum Virginisch Stendel-wurtz

905. Arethusa Virginisch Zweiblatt

906. Cypripedium Frauen-Schuch

Actæa *Christophs Kraut.* | Bocconia *Americ. Schöllkraut.* | Sanguinaria *Blutkraut.* | Podophyllum *Fußblatt.* | 572. Chelidonium. *Schöllkraut.*

4 *Stylo brevi vel nullo.* PAPAVERINÆ *Sive* RHOEADES. MOHNKRÄUTER.

573. Papauer,   Magsamen.   Argemone. *Stachel Mohn.*

Cistus. *Cisten Röslein.*   5. *Stylo elongato.* CISTOIDEÆ *Sive* PERFORATÆ. BALSAMKRÄUTER.   Telephium *Wundkraut.*

Hypericum. *Johanns Kraut.* Ascyrum.

Tab. 40.

Classis XIV. DIDYNAMIA ZWEYERHABENE. A. Gymnospermia VERTICILLATÆ MELISSENPFLANZEN

C. G. Geißler, Pinx. et Sculps.

Tab. 42.

Classis XIV. DIDYNAMIA ZWEYERHABENE. B. Angiospermia. RINGENTES. LARVEN-PFLANZEN.

C. G. Geyßler. del. et sculps.

b. Corollis tubipetalis CAPITATÆ. Plantæ CYNAROCEPHALÆ, DISTELPFLANTZEN.

829. Echinops. Kugeldistel. Polyg. Segr. 828. Gundelia. Saulendistel. Polyg. Segr. 830. Arctium. Klette. 831. Serratula. Scharten Kraut.

834. Onopordum. Vieh Distel. 832. Carduus. Distel. 833. Cynara. Artischocke.

836. Carlina. Eberwurtz. 837. Carthamus. Saflor. 835. Cnicus. Cardobenedicten. 837. Atractylis. Gitterdistel.

Sphæranthus. Kugelbluhme. 893. Polyg. Segr. 880. Centaurea. Flockenbluhme. Polyg. 3. frustr. Corymbium. Puschelbluhme. 895. Monogam.

Tab. 52.

Classis XIX. SYNGENESIA. ZUSAMMENGEWACHSENE. C.D. Polygannia frustranea. HELIANTHI SONNENBLUMEN.

C. G. Geißler. Pinx. et Sculps.   OPPOSITIFOLIIS add. Pectis T. 63. Amellus T. 76.

Sarracenia.   Sarrasine.   XIII. 1.   Nymphæa.   Seebluhme.   XIII. 1.   Aizoon. Eiß-Kraut. Tetragonia. Vier.X
578.   579.   553.   551.   Frucht

552.   Mesembryanthemum.   Ficoides.   Africanische-Feige.   540.Portulaca.   Burtzel.   XI.1.

Tab. 12.

Classis V. PENTANDRIA FÜNF-FÆDICHTE. A. Monogynia b. Monopetala. capsula intra florem.

172 Diapensia Bey Sand 178 Aretia Aretie. PRECIÆ d. ROTACEÆ. HUE BLUHMEN

179. Androsace. Hornisch-bluhme. 180. Primula, Auricula Ursi. Schlüssel-bluhme, Auricule. 181 Cortusa Cortuse.

182. Soldanella Pranzen Aglan. 183 Dodecatheon Meadie 184. Cyclamen Schwein-brod. 185 Menyanthes Nymphoides Biberklee, Kleine Seeblühme. 186 Hottonia Wasser-Viole.

188 Lysimachia Weidrich. 189 Anagallis Gauchheil 284 Swertia Duppel-bluom 285. Gentiana, Centaurium minus, Erdgall, Bitterwurz, Tausendguldenkraut.

205 Samolus Wasser-Bachbunge. 227 Chironia Chironie. 192 Exacum Africa Enoch Bitterkraut. 193 Sarothra Virginisch Bern Kraut. 190 Theophrasta Grne. 191 Patagonula Patagon 197 Ophiorhiza mungos 194 Randia Stachlichte Cacao 196 Plumbago Bley Kraut.

187. Hydrophyllum v. Borraginas. 192. Spigelia v. Asclepiadeae. 195. Azalea v. Bicornes. PRECIIS add. Limosella T. 43.
ROTACEIS add. Trientalis T. 24. Centunculus T. 9. Phlox T. 13. CISTOIDEÆ T. 30.

G.D. Gabler. Pinx. et Sculps.

Tab. 25.

Classis VI. HEXANDRIA SECHSFÆDICHTE. A. B. C. D. Mono - Tri - Tetra - Polygynia.

A. MONOGYNIA. 4. Monopetala nudæ. CORONARIÆ. HYACINTHEN.

B. TRIGYNIA. I. SARMENTACEÆ.

C. TETRAGYNIA. D. HEXAGYNIA.

E. POLYGYNIA.

Tab. 30.

Classis X. DECANDRIA ZEHENFÆDICHTE. B.C.D.Di-Tri-Pentagynia CARYOPHYLLEI NELKEN-BLUMEN

500. Dianthus Nägelein Blumen Gras-blumen 499. Saponaria Saffen-Kraut

498. Gypsophila Gips-pflantze 441 Bufonia 444 Mochringa Moh K.TIGYNIA 501 Drypis V.3 502 Cucubalus Schnall-blume

503 Silene Leim Nägelein 504 Stellaria Stern Flammelein 505 Arenaria Sand-Kraut 506 Cherleria Cherlerie 342 Alsine V.3

341 Pharnaceum 340 Corrigiola 96 Mœnhia 98 Holosteum 503 Queria 99 Mollugo 92 Sagina

529 Spergula Spörk-Kraut 517 Lychnis III.PENTAGYNIA Jerusalems-blume 519 Cerastium Hornkraut

746 Geranium XVII. 10 Storchen-Schnabel 516 Agrostima Acker-Nägelein

Tab. 29.

Classis X. DECANDRIA ZEHENMÆDICHTE. A Monogynia. BICORNES MOOS-BEERARTIGE.

G. G. Geißler. Pinx. et Sculps.   Add. Styrax, Citrus, Garcinia. T. 33. Haleria 69. Rhodora. 74.

Tab. 51.

Classis XIX SYNGENESIA ZUSAMMENGEWACHSENE.B.Polygamia Superflua flore radialo.ASTERES STERNBLUMEN.

C. G. Geissler. Pinx. et. Sculps.   DISCOIDEIS add. Osmites, Leysera, Perdicium T. 75.

Tab. 38.

Classis XIII. POLYANDRIA *VIELFÆDICHTE* B. C. D. E. Di- Tri- Penta- Polygynia

Tab. 40.

Classis XVI. MONADELPHIA *EINSÄULIGE* Plantæ MALVACEÆ *PAPPELKRAUTER*

Tab. 5.

Classis III. TRIANDRIA. A. Monogynia. a. Floribus spathaceis trilocularibus

Tab. 11.

Classis V. PENTANDRIA *FÜNFFÆDICHTE* A. Monogynia a. Monophyla

www.ingramcontent.com/pod-product-compliance
Lightning Source LLC
Chambersburg PA
CBHW060836290526
45792CB00006BB/1951